Goat Chinese Horoscope 2024

By

IChingHun FengShuisu

Table of Contents

Introduce

The character of people born in the year of the GOAT

People born in this year enjoy romance, fantasies, fantasies, and art, are constantly in need of love and protection, are afraid of failure, and prefer to look at the world first. People born in this year are extremely lazy. So you prefer to associate with wealthy people, dislike people of lower social standing, and prefer convenience. Because people born in this year do not dare to make a decisive decision and do not dare to do anything unless they are confident, they must carefully consider what they will do before doing it. This year's births are unregulated. Not suitable for business, craftsman, artist, or writer, or a career that requires creativity and artistic abilities. This year's babies are romantic. Everyone is drawn to the charm because it is sensitive, gentle, and affectionate.

Strength:
When you are given the last assignment, you will do your absolute best.
Weaknesses:
You tend to regret it aloud, no matter how minor.
Love:
People born in this year are frequently successful in love and outstanding at work. Finance and love are especially fond of fantasies about love going far in particular, love someone who likes someone who is always passionate about it. When you care deeply about someone, you will give your all. You are completely disappointed when you are disappointed. People born this year, on the other hand, are not afraid of love so easily that they can be duped repeatedly. It takes a long time for people born in this year to find their soul mate, and once they do, their love life is often long.

Suitable Career:
Jobs that help people are ideal for those born in the Year of the Goat. They can be social services

such as doctors, nurses, restaurants, hotels, handicrafts, arts and crafts, agriculture, or the sale of construction equipment. Construction contractors, engineers, designers, real estate workers, real estate agents, public relations officers, company employees, clerks, secretaries, lawyers, artists, singers, and actors, among other occupations, are all suitable for those born in the Year the Goat.

Year of the GOAT (Water) | (1943) & (2003)

"The Goat is not in the herd." is a person born in the year of the GOAT at the age of 81 years (1943) and 21 years (2003)

Overview

This year is another year in which you should take special care of your health if you are 81 years old. Because that will cause complications. Traveling anyplace should be accompanied by someone who can closely monitor you and alert you if you have any unusual symptoms. You must see your doctor frequently to ensure your health. You should also avoid having emotional disputes with your children or others. You should also avoid getting entangled in other people's troubles. The fastidious intervention with the children, in particular. To prevent ill luck and have good health, the chosen person should make time at the start of the year to get rid of misfortune and pay reverence to the god Tai Suai.

You cannot be eager for youngsters around the age of 21 during this year when every action will be carried out. It's due to the Thai Suai god's influence. Many issues are still pending and are not progressing as smoothly as expected. If you have the opportunity, pay tribute to the Buddha at the start of the year. Exorcising bad luck with a ritual might help ease severe misfortunes. This is because the evil star group "Kao Sua," the star Kiam Hong, and the evil star "Pae Uok" are harassing the house of fate, causing different troubles and hurdles. If you meet a problem and are unable to solve it, you should seek the advice of an adult. Take caution not to be misled by anyone. Be wary of roving groups. Because if anything bad happens, you will bear the repercussions as well. You should also be cautious of mishaps. The use of sharp instruments or equipment poses a risk of injury and bleeding. You should consequently prioritize your safety. During the year, however, the fortunate stars Hokchae and Samtai emerged to circle and radiate auspicious energy into the house of destiny, which was enough to assist in easing numerous calamities. In your studies, you will make progress.

The horoscopes of both life cycles this year are regarded to be another zodiac sign influenced combined in the Year of the Pig. You should make time at the beginning of the year to pay tribute to the Tai Suai Ia god to ward off bad luck and solve the terrible year, or purchase a set to pay respects to the Tai Suai god for the year at the Tai Siang Lao Kung Shrine. Be safe and create catastrophes from heavy to light to safeguard and protect the destinies in both lifetimes.

Career and Business

This year, you must strive hard to advance in your career and studies. Determinedly study, attentively research, and expand your knowledge. Today's world does not rely solely on work to exist. It is vital to have a wide range of information to apply in the future, and you must continue to study and obtain valuable experience. You should learn additional foreign languages if you have the opportunity. Whether it's Chinese, Russian, Korean, or Japanese, for example, it will assist in opening up more opportunities for jobs in the future. For the months when your studies and career are prosperous and progressing, they include the 2nd Chinese month (5 Mar. - 3 Apr.), the 5th Chinese month (5 Jun. - 5 Jul.) Chinese 6th month (6 Jul. - 6 Aug.), and Chinese 10th month (7 Nov. - 5 Dec.).

However, you should be careful during the following months when study and work will occur. Obstacles and problems include the 12th Chinese month (6 Jan. - 3 Feb.), the 1st Chinese month (4 Feb. - 4 Mar.), the 9th Chinese month (8 Oct. - 6 Nov.) and the 11th month of China (6 Dec. 2024 - 4 Jan. 2025) Be wary of being duped into doing something wrong by individuals with ill motives. When signing a scholarship contract, accepting a job, or applying for a job, you may be duped into being disadvantaged. When it comes to establishing a new career, entering the stock market, and making other investments, you must think carefully before making a decision.

Financial

The financial horoscope for this year is acceptable. Expenses are considerable, while income is a little low. If you are unable to discover a means to supplement your income. The most effective method is to cut costs. To determine if your financial condition is balanced or not, you must withdraw your savings and spend it to tackle immediate concerns. Gambling is not an investment that will endure for a long time. As a result, one should not be greedy in the goal of becoming wealthy quickly this year. It might make you even more impoverished than you were before. The months in which finances will decline include the 12th Chinese month (6 Jan. - 3 Feb.), the 1st Chinese month (4 Feb. - 4 Mar.), the 9th Chinese month (8 Oct. - 6 Nov.) and the 11th month of China (6 Dec. 2024 - 4

Jan. 2025) Do not let others borrow money or sign financial guarantees. Do not gamble, do not engage in trade that verges on breaking the law. For the months in which your finances are flowing smoothly, they are the 2nd Chinese month (5 Mar. - 3 Apr.), the 5th Chinese month (5 Jun. - 5 Jul.), the 6th Chinese month (6 Jul. – 6 Aug.), and the 10th Chinese month (7 Nov. – 5 Dec.)

Family

This year's family horoscope will be a combination of good and negative. Even if auspicious power is coming to visit, the wicked stars Heng Sua and Kao Sua will come to upset you. This frequently results in the safety of family members and engagement in lawsuits, senior citizen health concerns, and loss of property and medical bills for members of the family. The months during which the family will experience turbulent events include the 12th Chinese month (6 Jan. - 3 Feb.), the 1st Chinese month (4 Feb. - 4 Mar.), the 9th Chinese month (8 Oct. Jan. - 6 Nov.) and the 11th Chinese month (6 Dec. 2024 - 4 Jan. 2025) should use caution around metal gear and sharp things. Be wary of complications caused by disagreements with neighbors. Also, avoid escalating conflicts into litigation, and don't let your short temper damage your feelings. Great individuals are parents who put their faith in their children and think carefully because they know how to live.

Love

Even this year will be nice and lovely in terms of the teen's love life. The opposing sex is eager to get closer. However, it is founded on uncertainty. You must be wary of being duped. This year, however, you should remain cool and listen carefully. It will take time to establish how serious your kind remarks are. Please study and comprehend each other thoroughly. You must avoid interfering or being finicky in the affairs of your children and grandkids for this year's senior fortune teller. As always, the children will respect and adore you. During the months when love problems will occur, they include the 12th Chinese month (6 Jan. - 3 Feb.), the 1st Chinese month (4 Feb. - 4 Mar.), the 9th Chinese month (8 Oct. Jan. - 6 Nov.) and the 11th Chinese month (6 Dec. 2024 - 4 Jan. 2025)

Be wary of disputes. Avoid becoming engaged in your friends' love affairs, and avoid attending dangerous entertainment locations.

Health

Both fates are in poor health this year. Teenagers frequently suffer from headaches, are easily sensitive to the air, and are susceptible to colds. Be wary of allergies, infectious infections, and other hazards such as injury from sharp objects. You should also limit meals with a cooling effect, such as ice, squash, watermelon, grass jelly, and so on. For the elderly It is easy to become ill, so get adequate rest and eat foods that are simple to digest and beneficial. Be wary of concealed ailments that appear unexpectedly. You should locate someone to follow when you go out or wherever.

Be careful, you may feel dizzy, and cause you to slip and fall. During the months that fateful people in both life cycles must pay special attention to their health, namely the 12th Chinese month (6 Jan. - 3 Feb.), the 1st Chinese month (4 Feb. - 4 Mar.) 9th Chinese month (8 Oct. - 6 Nov.) and 11th Chinese month (6 Dec.

2024 - 4 Jan. 2025) to be more careful of accidents while traveling. Including doing various activities.

Year of the GOAT (Wood) | (1955) & (2015)

"The GOAT in a herd" is a person born in the year of the GOAT at the age of 69 years (1955) and 9 years (2015)

Overview

This is an excellent moment to invest, according to the horoscope for seniors. It is appropriate to identify a close heir to take over the business after you, your children, and grandkids join the work or an assistant to help manage the investment. Young individuals with strong physical abilities and work experience will be more effective. This year, the overall direction of work and trade is expected to rise. However, it will happen gradually. There are numerous methods to gain money by investing in various sectors. Your birth year, however, is afflicted by the bad constellations Kao Sua and Dao Pae Aok since it is another year that inherits the clashing force of the Year of the Dragon (2024). This will have an impact on the work-planned business will face challenges. You must carefully consider and assess the circumstances. You will lose both your money and your reputation if you make the incorrect decision. The second issue is health, and you must be extra cautious about accidents when at work and traveling. The next issue is having disagreements. Because he frequently encountered things that irritated him so much that he couldn't help but condemn them. However, it will happen gradually. There are numerous methods to gain money by investing in various sectors. Your birth year, however, is afflicted by the bad constellations Kao Sua and Dao Pae Aok since it is another year that inherits the clashing force of the Year of the Dragon (2024). This will have an impact on the work-planned business will face challenges. You must carefully consider and assess the circumstances. You will lose both your money and your reputation if you make the incorrect decision. The second issue is health, and you must be extra cautious about accidents when at work and traveling. The next issue is having disagreements. As a result, avoid becoming entangled in other people's issues and refrain from criticizing your children or grandkids. The following issue is the loss of property. Both from stolen or destroyed items.

This year, people born around the age of nine will encounter emotions of impatience and anger. Furthermore, they have a more private world and prefer to concentrate on technology and the objects around them. As a result, disagreements with individuals close to us are common. If you must travel overseas, you should use greater caution. This includes the need to be more cautious about traffic accidents. To fend against disasters and make apologies to the Tai Suai god, parents should take their children to pay tribute to the Buddha at the start of the year. To seek His Majesty's blessing to keep your children safe and make them lighter.

The horoscopes of both life cycles this year are regarded to be another zodiac sign influenced combined in the Year of the Pig. You should make time at the beginning of the year to pay tribute to the Tai Suai Ia god to ward off bad luck and solve the terrible year, or purchase a set to pay respects to the Tai Suai god for the year at the Tai Siang Lao Kung Shrine. To safeguard and protect the destiny in both lifetimes, be safe, and create disasters ranging from heavy to light.

Career and Business

This year's work, including business, has been turbulent. Seniors should seek assistance from heirs and grandchildren. It will aid in making employment more flexible. Both are cautious about interpersonal conflicts. You must match the appropriate individuals to the right jobs. Change stances to avoid confrontation. Before engaging in any action, you should exercise caution. Don't make biased judgments or pick and choose what you like and dislike. Because making the wrong judgment will result in harm. This year, youngsters must study more diligently. To improve, always revisit teachings. However, if you enter a month that is not favorable to you, parents should intensify and punish their children more strictly. During the months when the study, work, and business of the destined person in both life cycles will encounter many obstacles and problems, namely the 12th Chinese month (6 Jan. - 3 Feb.), the 1st Chinese month (4 Feb. - 4 Mar.) 9th Chinese month (8 Oct. - 6 Nov.) and 11th Chinese month (6 Dec. 2024 - 4 Jan. 2025) that seniors should avoid entering stocks and Various investments. During this period, be careful of subordinates causing trouble. Be careful of conflicts in the management line. As for the months in which the career and studies of the destined person in both age cycles will improve, they are the 2nd Chinese month (5 Mar. - 3 Apr.), the 5th Chinese month (5 Jun. - 5 Jul. .), the 6th Chinese month (6 Jul. - 6 Aug.) and 10th Chinese month (7 Nov. - 5 Dec.).

Financial

This year's financial horoscope predicts adequate revenue. Gambling on the stock market or calculating your fate in other things has a larger risk of losing than winning. As a result, you should modify your mindset and avoid being greedy, especially during the months when your funds are prone to leakage, and you should plan your money management and various investments. Should plan your money management and various investments.

To be careful, including the 12th Chinese month (6 Jan. - 3 Feb.), the 1st Chinese month (4 Feb. - 4 Mar.), the 9th Chinese month (8 Oct. - 6 Nov.) and the 11th month of China (6 Dec. 2024 - 4 Jan. 2025) You must be cautious of current spending that may cause your liquidity to diminish and trigger asset loss. Also, avoid gambling. Allow no one close to you to borrow money or sign financial guarantees, and avoid investing in illicit enterprises. For the months in which your finances are smooth and flexible, they are the 2nd Chinese month (5 Mar. - 3 Apr.), the 5th Chinese month (5 Jun. - 5 Jul.), the 6th Chinese month (6 Jul. – 6 Aug.) and the 10th Chinese month (7 Nov. – 5 Dec.)

Family

Your family's fortunes are not looking bright this year. This is because the home is destined to be disturbed by the bad stars Kao Sua and Guang Chi, which will generate troubles in the form of fights between individuals in the house. Be mindful of your remarks, seniors, as they may cause children to lose consideration. As a result, the best thing you can do is act as a counselor, offering advice and blessings to your children when they come to you. You should not allow your emotions to take over, and you should stay out of your children's and grandchildren's personal affairs.

Especially during the months when families are likely to experience chaos, including the 12th Chinese month (6 Jan. - 3 Feb.), the 1st Chinese month (4 Feb. - 4 Mar.), the 9th Chinese month (8 Oct. - 6 Nov.) and the 11th Chinese month (6 Dec. 2024 - 4 Jan. 2025) Be careful not to listen to malicious gossip. Be careful of people in the house having conflicts and speaking inconsistently. Be careful of valuables being damaged, lost, or stolen. Especially during the months when families are likely to experience chaos, including the 12th Chinese month (6 Jan. - 3 Feb.), the 1st Chinese month (4 Feb. - 4 Mar.), the 9th Chinese month (8 Oct. - 6 Nov.) and the 11th Chinese month (6 Dec. 2024 - 4 Jan. 2025) Be careful not to listen to malicious gossip. Be careful of people in the house having conflicts and speaking inconsistently. Be careful of valuables being damaged, lost, or stolen.

Love

This year's love is rough around the edges. The mind is irritated and unstable, and it readily gets into arguments with people. You must be able to regulate yourself. Don't allow your marital life over the past 10 years to be how it was during the Cold War, with you frequently turning away from one other or having disputes about trivial topics. Especially during the month when love is quite fragile. Arguments often easily arise, including the 12th Chinese month (6 Jan. - 3 Feb.), the 1st Chinese month (4 Feb. - 4 Mar.), the 9th Chinese month (8 Oct. – 6 Nov.), and the 11th Chinese month (6 Dec. 67 – 4 Jan. 68) You should not interfere with the internal relationships of other people's families. Avoid arguments If you calm down first, the matter will calm itself down. Avoid going to places of entertainment.

Health

This year's destined person's health is not good. Ailments, both old and new, will plague the elderly in particular. Be wary of heart disease, liver disease, and high blood pressure. Be cautious of dizziness, tripping, and falling, which might result in harm or anything concerning. You must be cautious about concealed ailments. As a result, you should closely monitor any unusual symptoms in your body. If anything untoward is discovered, you should visit a doctor right away for a full checkup. In particular, the months that are not supportive and you must be especially careful about your health are the 12th Chinese month (6 Jan. - 3 Feb.), the 1st Chinese month (4 Feb. - 4 Mar.), the 9th month. China (8 Oct. – 6 Nov.) and the 11th Chinese month (6 Dec. 2024 – 4 Jan. 2025), Take caution with your drinking and eating habits. You should keep it under control so that it doesn't taste overly salty, sweet, or greasy. Take precautions to avoid food poisoning. Be cautious about road injuries. Injuries from sports or trips abroad should be avoided by youngsters.

Year of the GOAT (Fire) | (1967)

" The Goat in the Grass " is a person born in the year of the GOAT at the age of 57 years (1967)

Overview

Horoscope for the Lord of this Age. Because your birth year is another zodiac sign that will be influenced by the strength of the Tai Suai. As a result, many actions this year will need to be thoroughly examined before proceeding. This is because the house of Destiny is influenced by both the terrible star Pae Ook, the unfortunate star Thiang Sua, and the Ban Sua star, which distributes influence influencing work and business. Personnel management issues can lead to internal confrontations. The trading company frequently experiences swings and changes due to external circumstances outside our control. Financially, avoid squandering your money and avoid being hungry for wealth that is not yours. Do not respond to requests to participate in unlawful trade, such as piracy or product adulteration. Because if you are detected, you may be imprisoned unless you have a legal case, and you should avoid having difficulties with bad debt accounts. You should also be wary of any unexpected incidents that may occur to home members. Keep an eye out for health issues and other difficulties. While traveling, you need also to be cautious of mishaps. Another concern is the misinformation about the hazards of visiting entertainment places. Because, in addition to causing you to lose money and waste time, it may also harm your reputation and prospects. If you contract a contagious sickness, you will return home and cause trouble for your family.

Because the destiny of this age cycle this year is considered to be another zodiac sign in the Year of the Pig that is affected together. At the beginning of the year, you should find time to pay homage to the Tai Suai Ia god. To ward off misfortune and solve the bad year or buy a set to pay homage to tell your fortune to the Tai Suai god for the year at the Tai Siang Lao Kung Shrine. To protect and protect the destinies in both lifetimes, be safe, and make disasters from heavy to light.

Career and Business

This year's task will be difficult. It must be exhausting to work harder than normal. Because you can't get away from the uncertainties this year. As a result, you should work hard to establish and maintain positive connections with everyone you come into touch with. Work or company must be true, honest, and forthright. Don't be selfish and cheat a bit; it's not worth it. If you trust in the power of collaboration and stand on the foundation of sincerity, you will overcome barriers. But you should be careful during the 12th Chinese month (6 Jan. - 3 Feb.), the 1st Chinese month (4 Feb. - 4 Mar.), the 9th Chinese month (8 Oct. - 6 Nov. .) and the 11th month of China (6 Dec. 2024 - 4 Jan. 2025) Be wary of business competitors who use dirty tricks and bullying to harm. Be wary of children or subordinates who cause problems. Be wary of fraudsters who are seeking methods to exploit you and lead you to lose money, such as by signing employment contracts or accepting positions. You should pay close attention to the little things. Avoid being at a disadvantage.

Furthermore, there is a risk of being misled while investing and being wary of employee or partner fraud and embezzlement. As for the months in which your work and business will experience progress and prosperity, they are the 2nd Chinese month (5 Mar. - 3 Apr.), the 5th Chinese month (5 Jun. - 5 Jul.) 6 Chinese months (6 Jul. – 6 Aug.) and 10 Chinese months (7 Nov. – 5 Dec.)

Financial

This year's budget is in shambles. Keep an eye out for internal leaks and unforeseen costs. Be wary of subordinates or minors who cause difficulties and cause property damage. Furthermore, bad debts from clients will be discovered during the year. Working capital liquidity is also reduced as a result of this. Especially during the 12th Chinese month (6 Jan. - 3 Feb.), the 1st Chinese month (4 Feb. - 4 Mar.), the 9th Chinese month (8 Oct. - 6 Nov.), and the 11th month of China (6 Dec. 2024 - 4 Jan. 2025) During this time, no credit is granted. When old customers' claims are due, they should be processed as soon as possible. Stay away from gambling. Do not lend money or sign financial commitments to others. When investing, do not want money or believe in the illusions of beauty and luxury. You should also avoid responding to solicitations to participate in unlawful trading. Furthermore, the income-expense system should be balanced to avoid a shortage of liquidity. As for the months in which your finances are flowing smoothly, they are the 2nd Chinese month (5 Mar. - 3 Apr.), the 5th Chinese month (5 Jun. - 5 Jul.), the 6th Chinese month (6 Jul. – 6 Aug.) and the 10th Chinese month (7 Nov. – 5 Dec.).

Family

There is a lack of tranquility this year. Because the house is destined to confront a brilliant and dark evil star attempting to infiltrate the family foundation, producing a loss of tranquility among the family. From property loss to issues with individuals in the house, illness, and bereavement for senior relatives. Especially during the 12th Chinese month (6 Jan. - 3 Feb.), the 1st Chinese month (4 Feb. - 4 Mar.), the 9th Chinese month (8 Oct. - 6 Nov.), and the 11th month of China (6 Dec. 2024 - 4 Jan. 2025) You should be more cautious about mishaps involving you and other people in the home, or about individuals in the house arguing with people next door. Threats from servants causing problems or causing harm in the residence. Be wary about thieves damaging, losing, or stealing your possessions.

Love

The love horoscope for this year is not favorable. Even little issues can quickly escalate into major issues, and there are several reasons for you and your spouse to be distrustful of one other. As a result, you should not take lightly talk from people who do not wish you well, and you should not allow work to keep you so busy that you have no time for family or loved ones. The greatest approach to building your relationship and adding sweetness is to make time to dine together at the table or go sightseeing together. The months during which you will easily encounter conflicts and arguments are the 12th Chinese month (6 Jan. - 3 Feb.), the 1st Chinese month (4 Feb. - 4 Mar.), the 9th Chinese month (8 Oct. - 6 Nov.), and 11th Chinese month (6 Dec. 2024 - 4 Jan. 2025). Be cautious and aware of your emotions throughout this time. Allow menopausal hormones to undermine a previously healthy relationship. Avoid going to various types of entertainment and avoid interfering with other people's family ties.

Health

This year's destiny is in poor health. You should start paying attention to food and beverage hygiene. Avoid drinking, smoking, and using drugs. You should also be cautious about liver illness, heart disease, and limb difficulties. When walking outside in high or low places, be cautious of being dizzy and falling and injuring yourself. Both must be wary of past ailments reappearing or of quiet diseases emerging and threatening to take control. Especially during the months that you need to be more careful and attentive, including the 12th Chinese month (6 Jan. - 3 Feb.), the 1st Chinese month (4 Feb. - 4 Mar.), the 9th Chinese month (8 Oct. - 6 Nov.) and 11 Chinese month (6 Dec. 2023 - 4 Jan. 2024). In addition, be more careful about accidents during work. or after taking medicine You should rest indoors rather than go outside.

Because there may be an accident causing
injury.

Year of the GOAT (Earth) | (1979)

" The Goat in distress" is a person born in the year of the GOAT at the age of 45 years (1979)

Overview

Those born in the Year of the Goat, who are approximately 45 years old, will face the power of damage when the Year of the Goat arrives in 2024. As a result, "Heng" is found to be another zodiac sign of the Year of the Goat. In the year influenced by this power, you must enhance your patience as well as your diligence and self-improvement. This year, there will be work on the show. This is because hostile stars appear in the house of fate. This will extend its effect and have an impact on the safety of the home members. Being bothered by subordinates or subordinates causes issues, resulting in misery, property damage, and loss. Keep an eye out for valuables that have been damaged, misplaced, or stolen. Don't be reckless regarding workplace and road accidents. There is one more thing you should be cautious of: you should be cautious with your own words. Do not insult or embarrass people by offending or speaking sarcastically to them. All of them are justifications for vengeance. Both should be wary of the devil's power. It will easily creep in and throw you off course. However, pressure and congestion will be felt in many areas around you. However, there are pathways to advancement that you may take to extend your job and branch. To boost productivity, you should plan for additional investments following the previously laid out strategies. Don't ponder about it; instead, invest. You don't have to listen to anyone's criticisms since a road of wealth will arise for you to follow throughout the month that favors work and business. Please work hard to strengthen and establish relationships at both the top and lower levels of the organization. People who have to go out to do business are included. This year, the boss has the authority to persuade subordinates to support him. There are prospects for wage modifications and promotions as long as you are diligent and persistent in growing yourself to deal with change.

Because the fate of this age cycle this year affects another zodiac sign. You should make time at the start of the year to honor the Tai Suai Ia deity. To fend against misfortune and solve a terrible year, purchase a set and pay tribute to the Tai Suai deity for the year at the Tai Siang Lao Kung Shrine. Be safe and create catastrophes from heavy to light to safeguard and protect the destinies in both lifetimes.

Career and Business

This year, a fortunate star, Hiang Bu, will assist in sending patronizing energy. However, because it is a combined year, you must be exhausted. That is, to be effective, you must work hard to grow yourself. There are prospects for advancement as well as compensation increases. However, the connection within the agency must be robust. Nobody can stop you from thinking, reading, going forward, or accomplishing something. Especially during the months when work and business are prosperous, including the 2nd Chinese month (5 Mar. - 3 Apr.), the 5th Chinese month (5 Jun. - 5 Jul.), 6 Chinese month (6 Jul. - 6 Aug.) and 10 Chinese month (7 Nov. - 5 Dec.).

As for the months when your work and business will have obstacles and problems, it is the 12 Chinese months. (6 Jan. – 3 Feb.) , 1st Chinese month (4 Feb. – 4 Mar.), 9th Chinese month (8 Oct. – 6 Nov.), and 11th Chinese month (6 Dec. 2024 - 4 Jan. 2025) Be wary of subordinates betraying you, causing difficulty, or privately slandering you during this time. Make a deal with caution or you will be taken advantage of and harmed.

Financial

This year's salary is fairly nice financially. Even direct revenue is still coming in routinely. However, when it comes to money on the gaming side, you must exercise caution. Even if money is rolling in, if you are greedy, your losses will outweigh your profits. Throughout the year, you will notice cash moving out in unexpected ways. You should have a backup plan in place. Especially during the months when the financial stars are in decline, namely the 12th Chinese month (6 Jan. - 3 Feb.), the 1st Chinese month (4 Feb. - 4 Mar.), the 9th Chinese month (8 Oct. – 6 Nov.) and the 11th Chinese month (6 Dec. 2024 – 4 Jan. 2025) Be wary of a lack of liquidity. Should eliminate unneeded costs. Find a strategy to supplement your income and avoid gambling, gambling, and fortune-telling of any type. Make no loans or assurances to anybody. Do not engage in illicit activities. For the months when your finances are flowing smoothly, including the 2nd Chinese month (5 Mar. - 3 Apr.), the 5th Chinese month (5 Jun. - 5 Jul.), the 6th Chinese month (6 Jul. – 6 Aug.), and the 10th Chinese month (7 Nov. – 5 Dec.)

Family

There was an unavoidable collision of forces in family issues. However, if you have a strategy in place for managing any auspicious happenings in your home this year, the auspicious energy will assist in easing many of the unfavorable energies. However, if no fortunate occurrence occurs, you should be extra cautious about events that occur outside of your expectations. Accidents and health issues in the house, in particular, necessitate strict attention to the health of the elderly in the family. Especially during the following months that you should be careful of special problems: 12th Chinese month (6 Jan. - 3 Feb.), 1st Chinese month (4 Feb. - 4 Mar.), 9th Chinese month (8 Oct. - 6 Nov.) and 11th Chinese month (6 Dec. 2024 - 4 Jan. 2025) Take cautious not to annoy anyone close. Because it may turn into a massive fight. Be wary of rash subordinates or youngsters who cause problems and destruction. You should also pay attention to safety and install burglar alarms or CCTV cameras to deter intruders.

Love

This year has seen monsoon waves in your romantic life. You and your partner frequently disagree, and each of you grows more outspoken. As a result, it is appropriate to accompany your spouse and lover to the temple at a peaceful moment to make merit and pay tribute to the Buddha. It will help you improve your love luck even more. Because the power of the devil comes to annoy you throughout the year of love. Be wary of engaging in vices or diverting from the path that may cause little issues to become major issues. The risk comes when you fall temporarily in love. You may acquire mementos that are a sickness of love, or some of you may be afflicted with a serious disease, in addition to squandering money and time. It will harm your reputation and prospects. Especially during the 12th Chinese month (6 Jan. - 3 Feb.), the 1st Chinese month (4 Feb. - 4 Mar.), the 9th Chinese month (8 Oct. - 6 Nov.), and the 11th month of China (6 Dec. 2024 - 4 Jan. 2025) It urges the Lord of Destiny to be mindful, regulate himself, and avoid triggers that can produce disputes. Be wary of a third party arriving and causing a schism in the family. You must also refrain from acting as a third party in other people's households and avoid places of amusement.

Health

This year's health is not looking good. If your body is not in good health and you become ill frequently, you should focus more on cleanliness, drinking, and eating to boost your immune system. This year, both discovered the incidence of regular mishaps. So, whatever you do, please be cautious. Don't forget about safety. Especially during the 12th Chinese month (6 Jan. - 3 Feb.), the 1st Chinese month

(4 Feb. - 4 Mar.), the 9th Chinese month (8 Oct. - 6 Nov.), and the 11th Chinese month (6 Dec. 2024 - 4 Jan. 2025) Take note of any irregularities in the body. If you see a lump, experience discomfort in any region of your body, or notice any abnormalities, you should see a doctor very away. The disease is treatable. Furthermore, you should use greater caution when traveling and driving.

Year of the GOAT (Gold) | (1991)

" The Goat is extremely powerful" is a person born in the year of the GOAT at the age of 33 years (1991)

Overview

The horoscope of persons born around the age of 33 in the Year of the Goat. This year, as in previous years, every job activity demands prudence and clear thinking before proceeding, lest you get impatient in many areas. Consult if you are stuck and unable to discover a solution. An adult or someone competent and experienced will assist in resolving the issue and finding a solution. Because your birth year is another zodiac sign afflicted by the force of "Heng" this year, you are hot-tempered, aggressive, and lacking in humility and civility. As a result, you should be mindful of your posture and voice, as well as your ability to interact and organize human connections at both the top and lower levels, since they have consequences for your future advancement.

In terms of financial fortunes, there will be numerous occasions this year when unexpected costs will arrive and suck cash. As a result, investment should be approached with prudence. However, because the planet that circles into your house of destiny this year is Dao Pae Aok, you will be able to strive for achievement this year if you enhance your diligence and commitment. You should take your intended plans and complement them with knowledge and experience, and you should not be disheartened by hurdles. Diligence will assist in compensating for and filling up the gaps. The term "affected by brewing power" has two different meanings. If you're still good overall but being brewed, it might be disastrous. If the initial atmosphere is not favorable, then enjoy the brewing power of the year. Bad things happen. In terms of your destiny criterion, this year leans toward the latter, placing it under the year of impact. It will help you stay in a position where you will not be beaten if you add strength to never give up and grow yourself. However, socializing with pals this year. It is essential to keep a kind watch on you. If you do not check your carelessness and trustworthiness, you risk being deceived by friends who do not mean to be nice and surreptitiously defame, talk, or sell information. Those who do business should be cautious of being duped by fraudsters and creating harm.

Because of the fate of this age cycle, this year is regarded to be another zodiac sign in the Year of the Pig that is impacted simultaneously. You should make time at the start of the year to honor the Tai Suai Ia deity. To fend against misfortune and solve a terrible year, purchase a set and pay tribute to the Tai Suai deity for the year at the Tai Siang Lao Kung Shrine. Be safe and create catastrophes from heavy to light to safeguard and protect the destinies in both lifetimes.

Career and Business
This year will be a trying time for your career and business. As a result, you should seek to better yourself. Bring specific knowledge and skills to get the highest outcomes, sales, and revenue. Work should be done with honesty

rather than arrogance. Because doing so would just exacerbate your difficulties, and you will meet blocking and hindrance from people around you. Whether you discover additional individuals who are jealous or upset, even one person is an impediment. Especially during the months when your work and business will have many obstacles and problems, such as the 12th Chinese month (6 Jan. - 3 Feb.), the 1st Chinese month (4 Feb. - 4 Mar.), the 9th Chinese month(Oct. 8 - Nov. 6) and 11th Chinese month (6 Dec. 2024 - 4 Jan. 2025). Be careful of jealous and bullying people. Signing any official contract To increase caution Be careful of being tricked by scammers. In terms of entering stocks or making various investments. This year you should look carefully before investing. In addition, you should be careful of embezzlement and corruption by insiders or the accounting numbers may be decorated by the partner. Also, don't be greedy or you will fall prey to cheaters. For the months when work and business are prosperous, they are the 2nd Chinese month (5 March - 3 April), the 5th Chinese month (5 Jun - 5 Jul), the 6th Chinese month (6 Jul. – 6 Aug.), and the 10th Chinese month (7 Nov. – 5 Dec.)

Financial

This year's financial situation is a red flag. Income and spending frequently change and are difficult to regulate. You should comprehend the concepts of making money and limiting your spending. Excessive leisure spending, such as eating out and frequent travel, should be reduced. As a result, one strategy is to spend less and save more. You should also be cautious of unforeseen costs, especially during months when your resources are tight, and you should prepare ahead of time. including the 12th Chinese month (6 Jan. - 3 Feb.), the 1st Chinese month (4 Feb. – 4 Mar.) 9th Chinese month (8 Oct. – 6 Nov.), and the 11th Chinese month (6 Dec. 2024 – 4 Jan. 2024) Gambling is not permitted. Do not lend money or sign financial commitments to others. Do not participate in or invest in illegal operations since you may be caught in the crossfire, assaulted, and charged with a crime. As for the months in which your finances are flowing smoothly, they are the 2nd Chinese month (5

Mar. - 3 Apr.), the 5th Chinese month (5 Jun. - 5 Jul.), the 6th Chinese month (6 Jul. – 6 Aug.) and the 10th Chinese month (7 Nov. – 5 Dec.)

Family

The family horoscope for this year is a mix of good and terrible. Auspicious powers will visit you during the rainy season. However, the year of strife will send two evil stars to connect and stay with them for nearly the entire year, particularly the Bo Ha star and the Nine Moon star. As a result, you should be more cautious and sensitive to the issue of sickness and accidents that may occur in the home. You should also be wary of those in the house who are arguing with people around. Especially during the 12th Chinese month (6 Jan. - 3 Feb.), the 1st Chinese month (4 Feb. - 4 Mar.), the 9th Chinese month (8 Oct. - 6 Nov.), and the 11th Chinese month (6 Dec. 2024 - 4 Jan. 2025) where you must be aware of unforeseen incidents that can lead individuals in the house to be wounded. Be wary of servants who cause problems. You should consider installing a security system. This is to prevent others from stealing, and you should avoid friends who wish to take advantage and take advantage of you.

Love

This year's love is excellent and lovely. Because the star Tho Huai came to visit fate's dwelling. As a result, it is an excellent chance for single individuals to exercise their freedom to choose. There are several favorable periods throughout the year to ask for love, become engaged, or marry. However, if you have a partner and a lover, this year your love is sweet and you can opt to go on a honeymoon. Just be cautious of the effects of the troublesome wicked stars. Spread your charisma in the right places. You will unavoidably have troubles with folks at home, especially during the month when love is relatively frail and conflicts and quarrels are common. such as the 12th Chinese month (6 Jan. – 3 Feb.), 1st Chinese month (4 Feb. – 4 Mar.), 9th Chinese month (8 Oct. – 6 Nov.), and 11th Chinese month (6 Dec. 2024 – 4 Jan. 2025) There will undoubtedly be misconceptions. Attending social gatherings at various entertainment places should be avoided. Because it will be the source of further squabbles and sicknesses. You should also avoid interfering in other people's families as a third party. It will devolve into an everlasting argument.

Health

The intended person's health is not excellent this year due to the impact of evil stars who transmit their energy to annoy them. As a result, you should be cautious of the danger of bleeding from workplace accidents, sports, and unexpected incidents. Especially during the months that you have to be especially careful, including the 12th Chinese month (6 Jan. - 3 Feb.), the 1st Chinese month (4 Feb. - 4 Mar.), the 9th Chinese month (8 Oct. – 6 Nov.) and the 11th Chinese month (6 Dec. 2024 – 4 Jan. 2025) to be more careful about accidents. In addition, after drinking alcohol or other intoxicants, driving a vehicle is strictly prohibited.

Chinese Astrology Horoscope for Each Month

Month 12 in the Rabbit Year (6 Jan 23 - 3 Feb 23)

The Year of the Goat horoscope begins the year this month and gathers negative energy. Obstacles and job challenges that have been overcome are still unresolved. There will be a fresh repeat this month. There will be disagreements and debates that have yet to be resolved. While negotiating with clients, various issues arose that needed to be rectified. What you should accomplish during this month is to complete difficulties that need to be settled swiftly and to employ tenderness strategies to tame harshness.

During this time, blunders in work and business are likely. Both encountered difficult-to-resolve issues within the agency. Working with consumers during this period resulted in subpar results. You must strive to make accurate changes, even if you have a high quantity of orders to fill. Contract conditions that may result in fines should be avoided.

In terms of fortune, this wage is volatile. Gambling involves both profit and loss. If you are not very greedy, being thrifty is advantageous, and you should look for cash leaks. To avoid having to cope with additional issues and concerns. The family horoscope is serene. There will be an opportune moment to move into a new house, or an auspicious event will occur in the house. Love horoscopes do not go easily since neither party will be disappointed. A third party will likewise get into hot water.

Air allergies, colds, and frequent coughing and sore throat symptoms should be avoided at this time. You must maintain good cleanliness when it comes to meals, eating, and getting adequate relaxation. You should also be cautious of mishaps while traveling both locally and long distances. In terms of family and friends, at this time, you may encounter people who like to encourage you to trip or who have financial troubles. When it comes to stocks and other investments, be cautious since there will be issues with investment funds and accounting fraud.

Support Days: 4 Jan., 8 Jan., 12 Jan., 16 Jan., 20 Jan., 24 Jan., 28 Jan.
Lucky Days: 7 Jan., 19 Jan., 31 Jan
Misfortune Days: 2 Jan., 14 Jan., 26 Jan
Bad Days: 1 Jan., 11 Jan., 13 Jan., 23 Jan., 25 Jan.

Month 1 in the Dragon Year (4 Feb 23 - 5 Mar 23)
This month, your fate shifts to the front lines of conflict. As a result, the horoscope travels downward vertically. The horoscope's road is hard and uneven, and obstacles and issues develop gradually. During this time, you should be extra cautious in all of your work activities. You should not be impatient and use your emotions to magnify a minor issue into a major one needlessly, such as hitting a dead end for no reason.

This salary fate is not favorable. Income is minimal, but costs are catching up and eventually overwhelming it. You are likely to lose your fortune in the middle of the month. If you are excessively greedy, you may easily fall victim to fraudsters. If you have income this month, you must save and set aside money in case of an emergency. It's not a good idea to gamble. Make no loans to anyone or sign any promises. You will risk criminal prosecution if you invest in illicit firms. Workplace conflicts are common. You must look after your immediate group. You may have to let go in some cases. This month is referred to as getting overly engaged in other people's concerns. When signing contracts and other paperwork, you must be extra cautious and suspicious of being put at a disadvantage. In terms of beginning a new employment, participating in joint ventures, and making various investments. Because this is a bad time, you should stop for the time being.

The horoscope for the family is not favorable. Increase awareness of the elderly's health and concern against possessions being destroyed or stolen. Misunderstandings about love are common, resulting in quarrels and leading the mind to wander wildly, desiring to go outside.

Be wary of pursuing vices and fleeting love that will make your life unhappy. Your health is not excellent, and you should not be reckless with accidents.

Support Days: 1 Feb., 5 Feb., 9 Feb., 13 Feb., 17 Feb., 21 Feb., 25 Feb, 29 Feb.
Lucky Days: 12 Feb., 24 Feb.

Misfortune Days: 7 Feb., 19 Feb.
Bad Days: 4 Feb., 6 Feb., 16 Feb., 18 Feb., 28 Feb.

Month 2 in the Dragon Year (6 Mar 23 - 5 Apr 23)
A summary of each age cycle for persons born in the Year of the Goat in the Year of the Dragon (2024). You must still exercise more patience and diligence. Because your birth year is believed to be another year that has experienced the power of producing and being influenced simultaneously. As a result, many topics this year will need more lobbying than others. If you have time, you should pay respect to the Thai Goddess at the beginning of this month to fend off ill luck and solve the bad year. This will aid in the alleviation of calamities and

misfortunes. In addition, you should analyze and assess your efforts from the previous year, and determine a new course for this year to prevent making the same mistakes.

This pay horoscope makes a nice living. Money will come in from a variety of sources depending on how much you have invested. May you have the fortitude to invest when the excellent time of the month arrives. The answer will be satisfactory. Because fortunate power and the patron star are circling to visit this month. Work, especially business, looks to be a prosperous route. Many things are readily achieved, making them perfect for new investments, establishing employment, developing sales, earning, working persistently, creating work, and increasing money.

The family's riches are tranquil and have patronage power to visit. It's the ideal time to fall in love. For single individuals who are undecided whether to beg for love or to be unhappy and want reconciliation. The door of opportunity is open and waiting for you this month. The disease will not dare to infiltrate healthy, joyful individuals. Good relatives and friends will provide you with inspiring counsel that will assist your brain in finding the answer. To begin a new career, form a joint venture, or make other investments. This month is ideal for making new investments.

Support Days: 4 Mar, 8 Mar., 12 Mar., 16 Mar., 20 Mar., 24 Mar., 28 Mar.
Lucky Days: 7 Mar, 19 Mar., 31 Mar.
Misfortune Days: 2 Mar, 14 Mar., 26 Mar.
Bad Days: 1 Mar, 11 Mar., 13 Mar., 23 Mar., 25 Mar.

Month 3 in the Dragon Year (6 Apr 23 - 5 May 23)
This month, the general direction of your horoscope born in the Year of the Goat is expected to improve. Problems that used to be a source of concern will become less so. But there were still certain things that were not as desired. You are afraid of deciding since you are scared about your future and your back. This work gave birth to a new tale. What you should

do this month is, if you dare, take care of your heart so that you may be conscious and operate within your capacities. Some things must wait, and you should wait. If you strain too hard, you will make mistakes.

Be cautious during this period of work if you experience difficulties with complaints or requests from customers or customers who receive poor service. As a result, the decision was made to seek services elsewhere. The revenue for this month is moderate. However, one must be wary of unanticipated leaks and money losses. There is benefit and loss from riches, therefore you should not be eager for fortune. Within a calm family, you have the chance to travel and see relatives, as well as find time to do good together to deepen family bonds.

In love, avoid being naive and trusting people too quickly. But, no matter what, you must maintain good mental and physical control. Don't dismiss entertainment and temptation. Hot food should be avoided for health reasons.

Grilling meals should be avoided. Make sure you get adequate rest. Control your meals and drinks to keep them sanitary and healthy for your body. Be wary of gastritis, intestinal sickness, and other issues that might harm your health and weaken you. The fates of the relatives are bleak. When you're around pals, don't only listen to flattery; instead, delve into your heart. You must still consider various investments carefully before making them.

Support Days: 1 Apr., 5 Apr., 9 Apr., 13 Apr., 17 Apr., 21 Apr., 25 Apr., 29 Apr
Lucky Days: 12 Apr., 24 Apr.
Misfortune Days: 7 Apr., 19 Apr.
Bad Days: 4 Apr., 6 Apr., 16 Apr., 18 Apr., 28 Apr., 30 Apr.

Month 4 in the Dragon Year (6 May 23 - 5 Jun 23)
This month, the fate graph of persons born in the Year of the Goat continues to plummet vertically from the previous month. Work during this time is extremely unpleasant and stressful. You also come across the wicked star Huang Pui, and focusing on it frequently leads

to terrible calamities. As a result, throughout this month, you should make every effort to be merciful. When challenges arise at work, one must be patient and calm to overcome them. You should not express your feelings to anyone around you, even those at home.

In terms of employment and trade, confront the monsoon roadblock. Be mindful of being asked to quit before your retirement date. As a result, attentiveness and excellent behavior will assist adults in understanding the value of not pushing away. You may lose your riches with this wage. Be wary about money leaking out or being duped. Do not invest in unlawful companies for personal gain. You should cut back on unneeded spending to keep your cash flow available for other purposes. You should also not gamble, gamble, and assess your chance in various stock lotteries. Anyone who comes to borrow money, begs for aid as a guarantee, or urges you to invest this month gets just one answer: "No."

Arguments and property losses threaten the family's prosperity. Be wary of items being misplaced, damaged, or stolen, or having to pay out of pocket due to problems caused by your subordinates. Including the requirements for paying for in-home medical care. You should not boast or wear valuables to attract criminals. The loving side is affected by winds and waves. During this period, stay wary of temptations that may induce you to alter or change your mind. You must be strong and observant. In terms of health, you frequently develop colds or are readily allergic to the weather at this time. You should avoid hot meals, particularly grilled and fried items, and you should use caution when traveling. Starting new employment, engaging in joint ventures, and making various investments are all examples of new endeavors. Be cautious of corrupt individuals.

Support Days: 3 May., 7 May., 11 May., 15 May., 19 May., 23 May., 27 May., and 31 May.

Lucky Days: 6 May., 18 May., 30 May.
Misfortune Days: 1 May., 13 May., 25 May.
Bad Days: 10 May., 12 May., 22 May., 24 May.

Month 5 in the Dragon Year (6 Jun 23 - 6 Jul 23)
This month, the route of life of the Year of the Goat advances to meet the month that is the ally. Immediately, auspicious stars could be seen rotating around each other, gathering to shine. Your horoscope's surface is as lovely as a rainbow. Your career and business will be given a seamless boost. This month, you should focus on developing positive relationships inside the organization with both your superiors and subordinates, as well as demonstrating your expertise and talents to others around you. The leader will urge subordinates to assist and smooth the route to the future.

In terms of labor during this era, favorable stars will provide reinforcement, resulting in a smooth course. Adults get the opportunity to view the work. For people who do business, trade, sell rapidly, purchase swiftly, and profitably. Some people help to support and increase sales and profits. If there is an opportunity, you should seek out fresh investment avenues with the ability to pay out dividends as needed. In terms of fortune, this wage will be higher. But I'm still having no luck with gambling or fortune-telling. As a result, you should not risk investing money since it will be in vain. Be cautious, or you will tumble and end up in another trap. Furthermore, keep meticulous track of your income and spending. To keep the money in the family flowing smoothly and happily, anything unnecessary should be eliminated.

The love horoscope is easy to read. This month is also a lucky month for proposing, becoming engaged, marrying, or being married. Those born in the Year of the Goat who are still unmarried might plan for favorable days. You should avoid drinking, smoking, and using drugs for your health because they all impair and cause sickness. Relatives and friends can still assist. In terms of beginning a new employment, forming joint ventures, and making various investments. This month, you can make some investments, but you must think about them carefully.

Support Days: 4 Jun., 8 Jun., 12 Jun., 16 Jun., 20 Jun., 24 Jun., 28 Jun.
Lucky Days: 11 Jun., 23 Jun.
Misfortune Days: 6 Jun., 18 Jun., 30 Jun.
Bad Days: 3 Jun., 5 Jun., 15 Jun., 17 Jun., 27 Jun., 29 Jun.

Month 6 in the Dragon Year (7 Jul 23 - 7 Aug 23)
The horoscope curve has an upward trend for people born in the Year of the Goat this month. Work tasks, including business, will be patronized. As a result, throughout this period, you should focus on developing and strengthening positive relationships with everyone you come into touch with. During this period, you must be vigilant and meticulous in your tasks. Do not rely on or borrow the nostrils of others to breathe.

This wage fortune is still a profitable moment, and cash inflows from what you have invested will come in. It is also a time to enjoy the rewards of your effort, which will bring you joy and relief. However, regardless of how you spend, you should always save and divide your money into pieces. It is preferable to let time pass and live recklessly for investment or money or the family. Because no one will have a steady and predictable income. As a result, you should create an income-expense account and carefully organize your finances.

This month, while appearing stable, there has been little improvement in employment and business. However, if you do not enhance your vigilance, unresolved issues may not be resolved. There will be disagreements in the line of command as well. As a result, you should not intervene or interfere with other people's work tasks during this time. Within a harmonious family, you should take care of and accept responsibility for your obligations to the best of your abilities. Members of the house adore and respect one another.

Love is as new and vibrant as a fish taking in water. You will discover someone you care about to assist and support. This month can encourage love for single individuals. Hurry up and ask if you want to. This month, be cautious of difficulties with the gastrointestinal or digestive system, so continue to practice good drinking and eating habits. If you want to start a new career, buy stocks, or make other investments this month, you should first thoroughly assess the circumstances.

Support Days: 2 Jul., 6 Jul., 10 Jul., 14 Jul., 18 Jul., 22 Jul., 26 Jul., 30 Jul.
Lucky Days: 5 Jul., 17 Jul., 29 Jul
Misfortune Days: 12 Jul., 24 Jul.
Bad Days: 9 Jul., 11 Jul., 21 Jul., 23 Jul.

Month 7 in the Dragon Year (8 Aug 23 - 7 Sep 23)
This month's horoscope for people born in the Year of the Goat has led you down a perilous path in life. The fate criterion shifts and shifts. Make every effort to be more alert and cautious when engaging in diverse activities. Be wary of being assaulted or intimidated by persons who intend to inflict harm. This month, you should think about who you associate with and be selective. Beware of the wolf disguised as a lamb. Don't allow greed to take control, otherwise, you can lose your money. You

should also take care of your professional duties. There is no need to meddle with other people's affairs or tasks.

In terms of employment, avoid using words that will produce disputes and issues that you will have to continually settle. When working, be wary of subordinates who are dishonest or make blunders that may upset you. Furthermore, while signing a contract document or doing any legally binding act, you must read it thoroughly and not be hasty, so that there are no regrets. Starting a new career or making various investments during this month is not yet viable, therefore it is best to wait.

For this pay fortune, money is lost. You should not gamble or invest in dangerous firms. Make no loans or financial commitments. Conflicts in the family should be avoided. Be aware of minors in the house causing disturbance or getting into fights with neighbors. Be mindful of valuables being stolen or misplaced. There will be problems in love, a third party will arrive in the midst, and running away will make your relationship even more turbulent. While traveling, be cautious of bronchitis, lung illness, venereal disease, and accidents. This month makes it tough to trust relatives and friends.

Support Days: 3 Aug., 7 Aug., 11 Aug., 15 Aug., 19 Aug., 23 Aug., 27 Aug., 31 Aug.
Lucky Days: 10 Aug., 22 Aug.
Misfortune Days: 5 Aug., 17 Aug., 29 Aug.
Bad Days: 2 Aug., 4 Aug., 14 Aug., 16 Aug., 26 Aug., 28 Aug.

Month 8 in the Dragon Year (8 Sep 23 - 7 Oct 23)
The fate of people born in the Year of the Goat will be devoid of perils this month. Life's path is now smoother and brighter. However, certain issues and roadblocks persist. During this period, you should employ honesty and sincerity to solve the remaining difficulties.

This month's budget is modest. To obtain the money you seek, you must be persistent in your quest. However, there is a possibility of receiving more funds from earlier investments and present activities.

Even if there are still storms at work, if you truly aim to solve problems, you will be able to conquer them. Whatever happens, you should push your growth in new ways. Both boost confidence while investing or conducting business. You will be successful and get excellent outcomes. In terms of family harmony, long-distance visitors will be visiting and delivering excellent news at this time.

The general state of health is excellent. However, be cautious of mishaps and injury to your hands or legs. This includes being cautious about getting injured by sharp items or electrical appliances.

Your love horoscope is not favorable. You should not dispute with your sweetheart, or you should compromise to avoid numerous disagreements. Relatives who are stranded will receive good cooperation and aid, and they may obtain useful counsel during this time.

Investing in stocks and other types of investments is doable, but you should select a low-risk option. Even if the return is minimal, the risk of loss is minimal.

Support Days: 4 Sep, 8 Sep., 12 Sep, 16 Sep, 20 Sep., 24 Sep., 28 Sep.
Lucky Days: 3 Sep., 15 Sep., 27 Sep.
Misfortune Days: 10 Sep., 22 Sep.
Bad Days: 7 Sep., 9 Sep., 19 Sep., 21 Sep.

Month 9 in the Dragon Year (8 Oct 23 - 6 Nov 23)
This month, the path of your life has taken a negative turn. Because destiny expands outside the alliance zone, it discovers the ability to incite blame. This month has half of the good and three parts of the terrible. Even though there are still decent walking paths. However, when you act, you discover that your power is insufficient, and things do not go as planned. What you should do this month is postpone investing and instead examine and wait to see how the scenario around you develops. Although everything appears to be moving slowly certain things must wait. It's

preferable to being impatient and making mistakes that cause harm.

Obstacles were experienced in terms of commerce and business throughout this era, no matter what. You must exert effort to progress. You simply need to be more cautious and find a technique to avoid errors. Be wary of being duped, used, or trapped by a contract that forces you to struggle. This is not a decent pay. There will be property damage. As a result, superfluous costs should be minimized, and your savings should be increased to prepare for unforeseen needs. As a result, you may become trapped and unable to go forward. Also, do not lend money or sign financial assurances to anyone. You should also not gamble, speculate, or attempt to quantify your riches in any manner.

The criteria for keeping an eye out for lost, damaged, or stolen assets is the family horoscope. When in love, avoid vices and attend places of amusement since they will have an impact on the relationship. In terms of health, keep an eye out for heart disease, high blood pressure, and accidents while traveling. Be aware of being slandered, deceived, or targeted by evil persons if you have family or friends. It is because of what you say that you may offend someone. As a result, please be quiet throughout this period. There is a potential that you may be duped into engaging in joint ventures and different investments during this period. Don't get taken in by flattering phrases.

Support Days: 2 Oct., 6 Oct., 10 Oct., 14 Oct., 18 Oct., 22 Oct., 26 Oct, 30 Oct.
Lucky Days: 9 Oct., 21 Oct.
Misfortune Days: 4 Oct., 16 Oct., 28 Oct.
Bad Days: 1 Oct., 3 Oct., 13 Oct., 15 Oct., 25 Oct., 27 Oct.

Month 10 in the Dragon Year (7 Nov 23 - 6 Dec 23)

This month, the fate of individuals born in the Year of the Goat enters the realm of the alliance. A constellation of fortunate stars is also orbiting you to encourage and assist you. It contributes to numerous positive changes. Work direction - business will find a way to thrive. During this time, you should opt to move forward with projects that you have already planned to become operational as soon as feasible to obtain a response that is not disappointing. Furthermore, you may need to modify the system or discard previous concepts that no longer make sense. Always strive to improve yourself and learn new things to overcome difficulties.

It's time for the tide to come in on business and business. Grab it as soon as possible. Please work hard to produce outcomes, improve sales, boost output, or increase investment. All of this will result in money constantly pouring into your pocket. This work phase will see a shift to a new appearance. A good opportunity has presented itself. You should seize it fast and not let it go away. This pay horoscope is lucrative in terms of both direct and extra money, and you will also benefit from windfalls.

The horoscope of the family is tranquil and gets auspicious energy to encourage it. You may receive positive news or hear about the success of individuals in your home. In terms of love, the road is covered with rose petals this month. Those whose hearts are still open will meet the person they have been looking for. Those who have a trapped marriage will locate a partner who will aid and collaborate nicely. In terms of health, you will only have mild diseases as a result of shifting weather conditions. You must obtain adequate rest to enhance your immune system. Speak only when required about family and friends, both good and negative. This month, you might not believe it with your whole heart. Take caution not to feel unhappy because you were duped. For starting a new career, investing in stocks, and making other types of investments. There is enough guidance at this point to take action. However, please double-check your readiness before investing.

Support Days: 3 Nov., 7 Nov., 11 Nov., 15 Nov., 19 Nov., 23 Nov., 27 Nov.
Lucky Days: 2 Nov., 14 Nov., 26 Nov.
Misfortune Days: 9 Nov., 21 Nov.
Bad Days: 6 Nov., 8 Nov., 18 Nov., 20 Nov., 30 Nov.

Month 11 in the Dragon Year (7 Dec 23 - 5 Jan 24)
This month, the fate requirements have shifted back to satisfy the line of punishment. As a result, many things that were going well had to suddenly come to a halt. During this phase, business affairs are like a little boat drifting against the river, desiring to progress but going backward, causing shame and being scared of an unforeseen turn of events. During this month, you should exercise caution in anything you undertake. Don't be too quick. Your job will suffer as a result.

In terms of work, be wary of subordinates or subordinates who may cause difficulty. Signing certification in any contract agreement during this period should be done with caution. When accepting or ordering work, speak effectively to avoid errors or harm. You should not neglect minor details that might lead to major issues in the future. Furthermore, you should be wary of being bullied or manipulated by those with evil motives.

This month's finances are volatile, therefore it's recommended not to increase your investments since gambling is risky. You should carefully manage the liquidity of your working capital, assigning one part for savings, one for investing, and another for prudent consumption. If your family fortune is not favorable, you will face turbulence and long-term disagreements. Be wary of being misunderstood by persons who deceive you in love. You must maintain solid control over your feelings and your conduct. This will aid in dispute resolution

This month, keep an eye out for heart disease and liver illness. It is preferable if you pay more attention to your diet and exercise regularly, as this will assist your body in becoming more immune and stronger. Be wary of being slandered behind your back by family and friends. It is best to avoid starting a new career. This month is not a good time to invest in stocks and other types of assets. Be cautious while modifying accounting numbers.

Support Days: 1 Dec., 5 Dec., 9 Dec., 13 Dec., 17 Dec., 21 Dec., 25 Dec, 29 Dec.
Lucky Days: 8 Dec., 20 Dec.
Misfortune Days: 3 Dec., 15 Dec., 27 Dec.
Bad Days: 2 Dec., 12 Dec., 14 Dec., 24 Dec., 26 Dec.

Amulet for The Year of the Goat
"The god Uai Tho protects against bullies."
This year, those born in the Year of the Goat should set up and worship sacred things. Place "The Goddess of Uai Tea Prevents Bullies" on your work desk or cash register table to improve your fortune. To request His Majesty's strength and authority to assist in protecting us from harm and to expand His authority so that we can live in peace and pleasure. The task will be completed with development and prosperity. It will also aid in blessing the business so that it runs smoothly and successfully, giving serenity and happiness to the Lord of Destiny.

A chapter in the Department of Advanced Feng Shui discusses the gods who will come to stay in the Mia Keng (house of fate) during their annual visit. Which is a deity who may bring both good and bad to the person of that year's fate. When this occurs, worshiping will increase your luck with the god who comes to reside in the year of your birth. As a result, it is seen to be advantageous and affect you the most to rely on His Majesty's power to assist and safeguard you while your destiny is sinking and there is tragedy to be relieved. At the same time, allow him to motivate you to make your business run smoothly and provide you and your family success and prosperity.

Bi is the zodiac sign of those born in the year of the Goat or Mia Keng (destiny house). This year, there are many challenges that you will have to deal with. There was a trade downturn. Furthermore, his birth year falls into the "Heng" digit, putting him at risk of persecution from those close to him. Someone arrived to steal the wealth. You must also avoid being sued in a lawsuit. Be wary of little confrontations that can quickly escalate into major issues. It's better to ponder before speaking and then act this year. Because your finances are not flowing easily, you should stop from additional investment and gambling on numerous topics. The loving part is lonely. Don't put too much pressure on the other person. If you want to improve your health, you should put up sacred artifacts and wear fortunate pendants. "Thep Uai is discouraged to protect against misfortunes" to beg His Majesty's authority and power to aid in the prevention of calamity. Encourage employment and business to develop and grow. Good fortune, money, health, tranquility, and happiness.

Phra Skanta Bodhisattva, also known as "Bodhisattva Ui Tho" in Chinese, is one of the major Bodhisattva gods. Its role is to preserve Buddhist temples and communities. Characteristics of Phra Uai Tho He will wear the Suvarna Armor and the Great Mongkut in both hands, carrying the magical Vajrakatha (iron baton) in the posture of holding the Vajra Kata (iron baton). His stance is aristocratic and well-balanced. This Vajrakathaw is used to destroy wicked demons and other bad creatures. The figure of Bodhisattva Uai Tho is usually placed behind Maitreya Bodhisattva (Phra Sangkaccaya), with his face toward the temple or temple. It represents riches and success. The worshiper will be rescued from calamity and will be blessed with pleasure and prosperity. May your wishes be granted with fortunate blessings.

Those born in the Year of the Goat should also wear auspicious jewelry. Wear "Thep Uai Tho protects against bullies" around your neck or take it with you as you leave the house, both close and far. Prosperity and growth in commerce and trade are required for the owner of his destiny to be filled with money and auspicious places. The family is pleased all year, which leads to more efficiency and effectiveness, as well as speedier results than ever before.

Good Direction: Northwest, Southwest, and East
Bad Direction: Northeast
Lucky Colors: Cream, Gold, Yellow, and Brown.
Lucky Times: 11.00 – 12.59, 13.00 – 14.59, 21.00 – 22.59.
Bad Times: 01.00 – 02.59, 19.00 – 20.59., 23.00 – 00.59

Good Luck For 2024

www.ingramcontent.com/pod-product-compliance
Lightning Source LLC
Chambersburg PA
CBHW021128130726
47988CB00003B/1202